Always,

The End

Brendan
Tripp

EPB-BT-025
an
ESCHATON BOOK
from

ESCHATON™
PRODUCTIONS, INC.

http://EschatonBooks.com

ISBN 978-1-57353-025-5

STRANGE DAYS LEANING BAD

1
abysmal stratagems
conducting negativity
the current is unleashed
all circuits flood with dark
pain pulses down the pathways
clouds gather, forming storms
a shadow takes tomorrow
breaking down the modes of trust

2
too much flowing outward
too little in
the rabid madness of the heights
hurls violence down
none are safe here
we hear the rumors on the winds
and find no shelter in the place
as destruction seals its grip

3
long from the voice maintained
it is different
latched to old fonts
we welcome entry from that side
and open up the gates in greeting
yet watch for danger
as once before
those nightmares spilled into this light

4
lost in spinning
here run sensations of the wheels
as cycles turn in cycles
and gravitation forms a weave
these days are meshing
each a cog which moves all else
we seek controlling
but can not reach around the whole

5
too many yokes demanding
too many mantles to be worn
and roles be played upon this stage
whose superimpositions
make us wonder which is when
and what is where within the grid
which spreads dimensions
beyond the limits of our ken

THE HELL WHICH THEMES THE DAY

tremors cross chaos
nightmares arise
we can not focus
we can not be
too many vectors press on I
making for implosion
rushing, falling, ever in
scrambled
untranslated
gone to random
spread through spectrums
shaken, stirred, and set

      fleeing
      flight
      and distance
      these are need
      these the want
      our escaping never felt
      never captured
      never deigned to be
      far flung
      delivered
      taken off from meshing gears
      run in destruction's way

give the darkness
pull the night a womb around
cower in its ebon warmth
hide from day
so cruel
so mad
so filled with evil
degradation and defiled
torturers with blades and chain
smashing us
killing us
erasing all observing eyes

      pain
      anguish and its agonies
      these erupt
      flow in currents through the heart
      burst as fire within the mind
      and sear the spirit black
      we ache for doors
      for seams, for cracks
      for portals that would lead away
      from crushing worlds
      this place of man
      and into gardens of the light

UNEASE BETWEEN THESE GOINGS

1
in abstract reeling
there becomes decline
without enumeration
denied the combination
or even clues
2
we stand before the mountain
murmuring soft its myths
we search the seam of sealing
the point where we might find
an entry, an exit
the wings by which to fly
3
paused in transit
our grasp can not contain
all that the heart would hold
the reaching it would make
4
all our greeds
erupt in focus
all our hopes
blast into want
all our dreaming
settles into ash
5
impetus of number
held apart from core desire
within the chaos turned
a safety from these storms
6
I reach for light in rising
hoping to forget it all
the spirit lifts and soars
yet the form is messed and waits
the eventual collapse
and disappointing falls
7
dizziness enfolds
pressed, all vectors spill
at center, unyielding
history does not detail
nor absent us from slaughter

DISTANCE BEING, OUT OF SYNCH

storms intrude
great crashes split the night
as sleep is broken
dark divided
by explosive light

the late late hours
lurk suspended
away from all defining acts
they are distant
a world apart
and lure for all their solitude
to flee the world of man

so weak the form
we can not take the course of will
and follow through this darkness
in expectation
sleep bids anew
as warning of the dragging day
that's sure to come without

so wished, the fleeing
that would strip away all bonds
and make of daytime options
and not necessitated chain
which drags us down again

SICK, TAINTED IN OUR DAY

nighttime fragments into rage
we can not fill all needs
as demands fall ridiculed
    no counting
    no dream
    we are broken off from sleep
    held apart in exile lends
        good turns bad here
        hope curdles into dread
        in acid wash

going, friction flares
nothing is easy
nothing fits
we shed off reasons
and try to pare our sight
        never a focus
        maintains by will
        only though guile
        are these intentions channeled
        only through lies waits truth

now the trap-door empties
and the plummet has ensued
    another dropping seems
    we cannot synch with flow
    only mass corrupting
        here is that poison
        hidden behind eyes
    as such being fails
    we turn a cipher
    blank, beyond desire

everywhere is dying's trail
it leaves a slime unsubtle
to trace the leavings
of faith and bright belief
        no funeral, no pyre
        just rotting, vile decay
    before these shatter
    and all our hopes destroy
    hold off one fantasy
    a shining thing so frail

INTO ESSENCES OF THINGS

evidently exhausted
the days turn to whirl
nothing gets done
no patterns farm
as glitches amass
to threaten as theme

we wait the process
we wait how filing sets
but lose the record
everything now slips away
beyond intention
gone into modes of slack

the river glistens
beneath a near-full moon
it moves so slowly
we see its flotsam
as spirits carried
down into the sea

it does not suffice
to be herein
we skim the world most briefly
so shallowly entwine
to know it not at all
except by memory

how many colors merge,
how many shapes here mingle?
a shimmering surrounds me
of wood, of cloth, of flesh,
moving and motive
wild beyond some calm

we trace the pilgrimage
and seek its capture
all its stations we would ford
within the self
making greater in the whole
than any one alone

WITHIN THE CHIANG DAO DEPTHS

deep, amid,
the earth enfolds
swallows into darkness
into darkest heat
time devolves here
splits from meaning
we can not trace or gauge its path
as it meanders
darker, deeper still
to watercourses lost to age
and crevasses of firm belief
sealed behind the muck of years
unsuspected, not unknown
these footfalls bring them here
if not unto the light

mind spins maps of mystery
seeks to dig
if not defile
and plumb the promise of these myths
so neatly found in place
fantasy takes up the spade
to trace the hollow-sounding floor
all other exit
in search of those
whose presence need meet new found lore

and yet we leave
the grime unturned
the spot unmarked
beyond the fading comment
to strike the blinding light
and wonder if the days are wrong
for showing caverns under caves
and libraries removed from sight
or texts awaiting surer hands
we wait to see
what we have seen
we wait to know
all that we've done
yet hear those echoes hollow still
pointing deeper into dark

TOO LATE FOR WHOLENESS

taken in illusion
not enough
without success
even these sufficient things
are drenched in failure
tainted with the breaking hand

these seasons turn too quickly
we are whipped from one to others
far too fast
we can't maintain
a stasis or a central point
giving us a place to be

we have become
a vagueness
a shifting
there is no focus to our acts
but desperation
a panic clutching at our dreams

now is the moment
the nexus of the terror named
there is no fleeing
all vectors drop
all options fall
leaving us with no release

the world becomes hallucinations
we can not tell our goals from dreams
or hope from fear
or prayer
turned into a scream for death
a deeper darkness than the night

these weak foundations
are all we have to base
our every future day
we ache with dread
and doubt fate
will touch us kindly in the end

TRANSCRIBED FROM WHAT IS WHISPERED

the voice does not maintain itself
perhaps the channel's bad
perhaps the linkage
runs to some other grave
and not to mountains
like these we read

    still it echoes
    somewhere dark behind
    and structures reason
    that cannot yet be known

a tide is building
a swell amasses
somewhere over these horizons
distant but yet felt
as by its gravity it pulls
at subtle fibers of the soul

    when waves come
    the format changes
    the flood intrudes
    and wipes these hours from the map

nowhere is insistence
greater than itself
it huddles down within us
and guides a pattern unexplained
almost set in being
almost known in light

    this is clearer than before
    the outlines of the walls derive
    as surface struggles
    to break into new air

we bide the passing of the key
and access to the garden
it lies behind the metal gate
and asks more than we offer
yet its vector drives outside
and begs our concentration

    here the answer to the prayer
    here the freeing
    if only in the loss of worlds
    denied our every contact

ON A VECTOR TO THESE ENDS

evanescent stasis
derived from shiftings
   center will not stay
   chaos pulls with weight

who finds these dyings
to manifest in light?
   we can not recall
   yet we are called
   we know no sureness
   yet we are sure

even distance
does not hold peace
the fire now burns inside
and threatens ever
   Armageddon's flares
   lurk behind these eyes

contravening focus
reverses all polarities
   we can not be
   in worlds that are not ours

now no knowing is
now no beings are
the grey erupts and spreads
   cancelling the day
   a static over night
   which creeps and numbs and blanks

everything devolves here
like melting pictures
   photos in acid
   watercolors in the rain
      hearts coming broken
      or minds lost at sea

see the wall
it hurtles on
   we bear the motion
   we ride the trace
we last look on the here
thought flashes on ahead
      in the moment's crush
      shall passage be attained?

DECLINING BEYOND DEPTH

without direction
without a clue
there is drifting
there is movement yet unwilled
    the rudder is broken
    the meaning fades
    we ride on impulse
    awaiting explanation

now is the dark tide
now bears this heat
into the season
removed from purpose or intent

        time collapses
        nothing seems to fit
        the days stack up here
            and leave no frame
            by which to clear

these hours are all bled
we can not use them
they are dry and light as dust
and blow away so freely
    yet we're not free
    our hopes decline
    our dreams are tortured
    with visions of stilled flight

darkness,
I am weakened to you too
I fade at every corner
drift away through every crack

        the streets are strange now
        they only murmur names
        which are not mine
            these will not claim me
            nor be a harbor in my fear

    unknowing
    in blindness set
    an emptiness becomes
    a hollowness intrudes
    defining self
    defiling all

AROUND ONE CYCLE UNEXPIRED, AGAIN

1
another entry begs
directions to define
dictating a new ratio
unable to be set

    the image is yet lurking
    the words
    they spill like sticky blood
    poured out from bowls of sacrifice
    upon these flagstones here
        we trace these patterns
            (yet are broken
            systems failure
            steals the rest
            unable to retrieve)

2
grasp that nothing
an emptiness answers
    how are we to trust
    any function here?
    this is damning
    void beyond our reach
        taken from us
        cleared away

    there are writings
    which drift without a trace
            compositions
            dependent on a web
            which is decaying
            gone without a trace

an anger wells
we can't regain
these bits of us
that cruelly fade to naught
    this rage finds nothing
    and squares frustration's need
how to fight,
how to bend this to our will?
we battle with the decline
and curse the tide of change
    so why must always
    these fragments fade ere dust?

DEVOTION TO THAT ONE

search for her voice
down, somewhere within
we know it lurks there
    we glimpse it in the shadows
    and sense it past these bends
we wait for it to take us
and swing us through her will
    changing all things
    shifting stasis
    into modes of light
we have not seen her
these veils, for us, too thick
but trace reflections
in the sky and on the earth
giving outlines as a guide
and hints of where to look

    there is such difference
    between her way and ours
    such depth we can not hope for
    and heights we can not reach

    we stand on wasted planes
    and raise our hands in prayer
    that she might swoop down
    and carry us away

we ache so for her touch
which strips away the world
and all the madness of the race
    driving crystal
    into a diamond glare
    bright, unrelenting
    never to release
only in her comfort
can we be as one
only with her vastness
might we reach beyond this state
    knowing all dimension
    spanning beyond time
    being holy
        wider than existence
        richer than all life

WAYS OF FINDING WHAT THEY MEAN

1

wordless moanings drift on swells
    behind perception
    around the corner from the brain
they follow paths uncharted
originating from the void
and seem to force a context
where none from here is found

2

walls are built around the walls
moats dug around the moats
patterns of confinement spread
from simple dungeons
on to towers, cities, worlds
all meant for our imprisoning
within the blindness here

3

so many lies take form
so many fantasies pretend
    to be reality
    to speak the truth
    to show the way
but these are vapors
swirling from our grasp

4

static point
no vectors lead
this is inertia
duration set
    frozen to coordinates
    locked to position
    damned to dull persistence

5

what beauty can be made here,
what joys uncovered in this cage?
these irons rub texture on our wrists
the stones twist sinew, warping bone
this darkness hovers like a sea
that would rush in choking
and cover all with mystery

DELAY IS SET WITHIN

a never and more
a substance of dread
an aspect of putridness
an oxide of lead

a vision of spans
a gap between stares
a downside to emptiness
a home for the bears

a colloid ungelled
a vista unviewed
a distance distributed
a candidate nude

an unturned decay
an open decline
a regular distillate
a wish-granting mine

a form of respect
a side of the whole
a deep-held extremity
a stocking of coal

a rancid display
a hollow retreat
an entrance to visitors
a dead-ended street

a tin of regrets
an unearthly glow
a short form of uselessness
a dusting of snow

a volume unread
a construct unmade
a vacant accelerant
a due left unpaid

an old-time dispute
a journey forgone
a crevasse encountering
a road set upon

a cycle abrupt
a distaste expressed
a package of parakeets
a hope for the best

FOUL SHIFTING IN THE AIR

old blocks are altered
stale directions change
   these are not the same
   cycles have run different
   and the gears no longer mesh
      those voices now don't reach us
      their words just hum with wind

there is no touching pasts
the habits fall like husks
dry and not of use
our recall degenerates
from knowledge into symbol
needing some decoding
beyond iconic sheen

   no going where
   these used to be
   no being with
   those patterns
      only visions
      written from some other life
      which we now doubt was real

hearing echoes of the system
making promises unkept
placing will before the decay
   and lying that it matters
   hoping that the wish
   would substitute for reason
   and cause the substance shift

nothing inside
nothing out
we lose our caring
and live just in desire
the sullen ache
and low fire burning
which drives all things away

all our good entombed here
hid beneath cement and stone
   a grave for all intentions
   a crypt for every dream
   a mortuary for our hopes
      which now lie dying
      deep beneath these streams

WHICH NUMBER TAKES?

1
external whirl
all things change
nothing shifts
within
2
one focus
one stage
bound, unmoving
unable to form acts
3
frustration burns
we cannot reach
the world we see
the light
4
other sides
alternate lines
is this unstuck
gone drifting?
5
just like that
could we maintain
are those options
accessible?
6
temple grounds
crossing frames
we touch this
yet cannot stay
7
these goings are
the central thing
no wings have I
to keep aloft
8
the need too deep
the ache too hard
no balm will soothe
no resting comes
9
sudden voices
spanning worlds
they scold
yet point the way
10
these vectors pull
all ways at once
we can not follow
and fall behind

NOT IN UNSAID ASIDES

formulated in the leaving
directed from the line
crossed across the aeons' dance
and into empties
vast like caverns building suns
or planetary shells encased
    we drift
    lose by filling
    churn by deed
    it is the openness we sought
    the vista cracked apart and seen
    without retention

()

too much extrudes here
we can not maintain
it goes from flowing
and into reach
it shifts to culling
yet without recall
    now is that vision
    we chafe against its sand
    rub to rawness
    unable to describe what eyes
    may have known
    if not destroyed

()

who can take these things for us?
who can gather
all the little tiny bugs
which crawl across that whiteness
and dare their capture
or their process in the sane?
    it is not the way it is
    it holds no valence with the past
    we are in this
    at the point of chaos sparked
    between the aspects
    of what might be and what is not

BROKEN PAST ALL FIXING

enough
is enough
is enough
a change
is a shift
is a sway

and otherness appeals
and difference desires

    this is
    the central point of life
    this is
    the nexus of our lines
    this is
    the broken split awaiting

hard choices
scary scenes
we do not want the edge of this
we only want our dreams
    which fade away
    which drift apart
    and leave us naked
    weak and so exposed

it comes around
the play is played all out
and with its closing
comes the bleak

    grey
    everything is grey
    everything is empty
    dead
    deserted
    stone and concrete lapping steel

    we are not open to this state
    we fold and seek the darkness

within
are the reasons
without
are the fears
with every dawning
come horrors and more tears

INTO ALTERED VISTAS

another eruption
new explosions spread
we can not become this
    we fail
    and don't evolve
    decline
    and cease to grow
stale visions pull
old wishes die
yet unfulfilled

the hollowness rings hard
we hold an empty
deeper than the sea
    denied
    what we would be
    in need
    of everything
no traces linger
yet smoke still veils
against the seeing eye

sharper angles pierce
darker vistas call
with the force of fate
    we drift
    without real will
    expire
    while knowing not
through these ages was nothing built?
we're left with vacuum
clutching at insides

only habit drives us
the tide of breath
still stronger than our pain
    abject
    lost in sorrow
    too low
    to grasp the light
here comes the frantic
the panicked and insane
a totem for us all

WHEN POISON CHANGES GOAL

there it goes
into decay
there it shifts
into collapse
there it falls
into demise

        we cannot break free of this
        we can not attain
            escape velocity
        we stay in orbits
        which lead to fire

nothing allows
    the wings
    dreams spreading
    fantasy gelling real

all apart
all away
drifting in some matrix flow
too thick for movement willed
too dark to see all scenes
        no contact here
        no way to know

an aberrant intrusion
here comes hard light
splitting down the seams
cracking open eyes

        even with explosion
        some walls will yet remain
            so we are cursed
            damned to this chain
            and the shadows of all ills

now our sentience betrays us
    we awake in sleeping
    with answers we can't ask
now our convolutions twist us
    leading past the vectored course
    and into realms unknown

THE CALLING, THROUGH DECLINE

1
orbs align
jostle for precedence
within the lighting
the rays and beams of night
this, the unfolding
of what becomes the pulse
this, the pattern
of the vectors of the season

2
traditions play
become entwined
we take the issue
and fold it in recall
sorting out the seeding place
and which result expected
when sifting comes
beneath those lights

3
all aspects gather
awaiting unity
within the caldron
of labor, toil, and strife
there intents follow
the realer lines' demand
and drive through hoping
what mind's eyes have foreseen

4
cycles teeter
nearly closed
set but for last things
final elements await
the next revision
within geometries
which may not come to be
or may arise

WHEN FATED AND WHEN DAMNED

1
out of light
    extruded
through the darkness
    torn
in false joy
    elated
by the season
    swept
2
all these failures
here amass
they, building, mock
they, growing, twist
and turn upon the self
reviling it
debasing it
abusing it as to destroy
3
cruel release
whose brevity
folds back upon itself
redoubling the evil
of unavoidable returns
to the dungeon
to the pit
to the hell of deathless chain.
4
old patterns call
their lures of vagueness tempt
and draw out drifting;
images confront the mind
of other places
other ways
paths we were too dull to keep
when all things optioned free
5
such dharma comes
and this we must enact
creating karmas more like fate
on all these interweaving lines
some days now echo
as long befores
as though a script played out
without an element of choice

BY SUCH REMOTE CONTROL

sayers say something
which is not defined
    illegible
    unto the ear
    strange unto the mind

from this proceeds
        the what which is not
        the where which is gone
        the off which is on

as if it were
or had to be
or even was
    wherein the times
    decayed beyond
    the limits of retrieval

        not a genesis
        just an echo
           in recall
           bouncing walls

I have not the wavelength
no signal comes within
    static issues
    from every eye
    and every pore
    streaming unsteady light

late beyond intent
only lines
the stretching mode
    to what is distant
    and not received

        when locked on
        to being
        when aimed well
        at night
        when synched to
        the pattern
        when struck with
        delight
           then is the answer
           but never yet before

STANCES WITHOUT SCENE

nature encircles the seen
linear forms evolve
structure turns to stone
all is ossified
fast-frozen in the now

there are no alignments
we all go without
these needs are ever present
not omniscient
yet nagging still the same

such trace the borders
of the realms of being
carving the latitudes
that we can not reshape
once etched upon the globe

systems degrade and fail
intent grows distant, fades
pulses do not reach
their targets in the planes
devolving now to points

our doubt grows greater yet
our fear the chop on seas
spraying bits of dread
upon the face and heart
when seeking for a shore

never rises the dream realm
the crystal zone
the place delivered pure
too much rot taints this space
and pulls down to the mire

another cycle turns here
so many wheels in spin
that no pattern sings to mind
no grid opens the door
to clear perception's gaze

all these far aways
can not remove the curse
the mass of ages' building
which can only once be broke
within the chaos line

INFAMY IN THE MIX

1
interruptions
dent the flow
blades swing free
and sever nodes

2
a greyness hangs
a haze entombs
a pall is cloaking
these forms of day
beneath that dark
we sense a light
denied to us
by weight and chain

3
one vector points
and names the speed
velocity's needle
swings back and forth
with nothing constant
and nothing real

4
a line is broken
a cycle unmet
madness and greed
change all for the bad
with gravity's drag

5
into the cavern
into the lair
a piercing comes
with violence, rage,
intents of voiding
what cowers within
in raw naked fear

6
no statement of reason
no outlay of time
nothing left to make a life

RED PAPER TRAILINGS

new year
rooster comes again
my sign

> bang!
> in chinatown
> streets are red
> covered with paper
> detritus of bursts

> all these dragons
> many teams
> we follow
> see them dance staccato

> fortuitous
> our being here
> without forexpectation
> a way to honor
> the 12-year tide

other passages align
we are taken with the surging flow
into different space

> flash!
> an image forms
> the mind awaits
> the hard return
> which brings to us the known

> around and around
> we recall names
> none have meaning
> none arise

> spirit melds
> with hunger, need
> we sit beneath the high
> and take to us
> both facets

NOT ENCODED ON THESE PLANES

1
totality
diversified
breakdown
crumble
eternity
vastness
forever
decay
destruction
depression
existence
removal
conjunction
rejection
erasure
repugnance
terror
vision
futures
nightmares
crashing
expiring
divesting
dismay

2
these go on too strange
we can not grasp them
and take a meaning
they are not from here
their course is distant
far beyond the night

from center points
all these vectors flow
tracing lines through matrices
which are faceted with worlds
and carve out vague tomorrows
which wait their turn to dawn

it is the moment of the pulse
the instant of dimension shift
causing changes
making up the new
the font of horror
and promises of light

WANDERING OLD PATHS UNSEEN

a)
it does not echo back
enough

there is no follow
within its reach

its histories grow vaguer still
through passage of the years

b)
these reminders
touch hard upon the soul
of what might happen
given changes to the line
and what strange memories
might be stored here in me

c)
the pattern once maintained
it was the focus
the way of light
but so seldom is its kind revealed
that it is alien
and not of us at all

d)
new dimensions turn
folding out from common reals
blooming into untouched zones
which are inviting
to leave all we know behind
and track into the skies

e)
faint tremors move within the web
and cast an intimation

who was this that was before
by any other name?

the muse pulls many within her veil
again, perhaps again

FALLEN, WITHOUT COUNT

1
different names,
alternate concepts;
do they orbit
an unseen center,
do they maintain
a linkage beneath?

2
elements decline
the glue wears off
makes all unstable

3
we break against the need
hard, brittle
too much velocity
thrusts into contact
shattering the structure
fracturing the form
until not much is left
from which to make IDs

4
new systems
altered view
a vista comes in filtered
edited of truth

5
such idiocy flares
as blindness leaps,
the ropes pull limb from limb
severing context,
only dreams remain
and the wailing ache
which drives beyond today

6
outer frames met
we transmigrate to fit
shifting through these options
becoming one with each
yet being none

MIRRORS IN VAST ARRAYS ALIGNED

1
systems that we don't believe
words which raise suspicions
2
what echoes
produce the ring?
what reverberates
within the canyon?
3
a tide of violence
lies dormant in the breast
    don't push these things,
    they are set to spring
    at the slightest notice
4
this wall
appears too high to climb
these mountains
look too hard to attain
5
how we ache
to make our dreams come true
against these trends of dark
6
hollowness resides within
an emptiness which crawls
7
some sentience
is sensed beyond;
there is a veil between
and blindness which corrupts our sight
    what traces lines then
    in that other realm?
8
we carry symbols
are marked of clans
which have for totems light
9
without the pattern
there is no key
without the framework
there is no structure
or applicable thought

DISRUPTED FUNCTIONS IN RETURN

1
from other stances
the memories flow,
we see these histories
and try to now maintain
the structure they present
against the wearing grind of time

> so much has been forgotten
> so much is lost in days
> which swirl by in distraction

2
so many vectors,
so many roads;
we play the angles in the night
and dare the angels to appear
bearing the promise
which is not being kept

> a tide is surging
> it threatens us with death
> in drowned submergence

3
those intents have shattered,
the flow is broken
as fractures spread across the will
and patterns drift away
giving haziness to place
and question to all scenes

> these mists surround us
> cut us apart
> denying contact with the real

4
new depths greet sinking,
we are all lost souls in this pit,
too driven by these appetites
to fashion crystal sheen
and blinded by our ignorance
to find the path of light

> out on this ocean
> all shorelines are mirage,
> deceptions of the safe

STRUCTURES FROM GREAT GRIDDING

abstracted context
we pulse the wave
and open up into the night
   new lineage
   new frames

it is the center seed
other formats that we heed
seen in vistas
   not familiar
   nor apart

these lead us to delusion
within delirium kept
      and flash to distant spinning
      held in recall
      ready for the playback track

at this confluence
we see all influences meld
forming one theme
   which is denying
   which has no base

something alters all the states
creating artificial matrices
for these embedded knowns
   everything is thus a lie
   everything is gone before

we watch as all believing melts
beneath the hard and killing light
   this is the promise
   the end of every dream
   now grounded with the rest

who has nothing and exists?
who allows the wind through flesh
and walks without depression?
   it is the warrior
   it is the shade

into this distraction
enter with no pain
giving credence
   there the forming
   there the flame

THESE THINGS THEY'VE RETRIEVED

1
against the beast
against these walls,
what call is coming,
what trumpet blares?

there is insanity deep here
an aberrant current
which churns things at bases
and leaves all doubting

blocks are set on blocks
it is the system that we fear
something too stable
to allow for motion through

these talons are so sharp
he fangs still lust for blood
what creatures come to slay us
if we journey from this cave?

2
inability
insufficience
    these haunt
    these follow
disbelief
disregard
    these taint
    these poison
reversal
refusal
    these crush
    these mangle

3
such roads lead
and doors open
options are given
yet not maintained
    it's a chimera
    a trick within the haze
such hopes fly
and dreams flower
visions go empty
when seen by day

SPOKEN FROM THAT INNER SIDE

1
are these without exception?
there is a counter flow
the doctrines spin amiss
and we have no more reason
except to follow tides
and shift locale with season
only drifting on the ride
into foreign concepts

2
another thing insists
yet scrambles basic order
there is no control
all maniacs are free
the tone is within frame
yet echoes out of context
allowing only troughs
without correcting rise

3
bled without return
gone without replay
sent without renewal
into zones unknown
the boomerangs of essence
weaponry unarmed
which rips apart the sky
and takes down every number

4
where does arise the voice?
what corner issues answers?
we do not know these things
yet trail on all the same
into image forged
from alloys unassayed
given cross the lines
of realities defrayed

5
nothing here, nothing left
all faces blur distinction
as location cedes to speed
we are only in the whole
and set apart from being
run through a downward cycle carved
by repetition and resigned
by doom and fate to failing

A PICTURE OF THE PULSE

analysis fails:
too many systems

forms enmesh
lines array
twisting, weaving
leaving us stranded
unable to align

other signs
bring up revulsion
we are broken at the start
unable to clear

the going takes
and finds these gone
it does not connect
ringing hollow
against the steel-lined walls

heat escapes,
why not the soul?

the image changes
pressed by will
but will not shift
within the outer world

now it is knowing
as though it said
the mantra of deliverance

that stasis beckons
in idle lure
we can not find the structure
which offers up support
to issue flowers
blooming through the day

common cadence
breaking down the eye
unset to march

still the stillness
the words are lost
all the visions
drift away
leaving concrete
to bleed upon cement

PAUSED AT CHAOS' BRINK

a)
these distractions delay
and somehow detain;
from unsuspected corners
directions arise
and trace out clear vectors
on the stuff of the void
b)
no narrations suffice
we are lost without guide
given to rambling
scaling up the stones
which have fallen from the past,
and searching for old ways
c)
our vision fails us too
backgrounds become blurred
shifting and uncertain
every light comes filtered
by uneven mixings
of our intents and our fate
d)
this knowing is disturbed here
all our files are scattered
rearranged by winds
and the currents of the time;
nothing stays in stasis
long enough to frame
e)
the chasm offers solace
and invites the leap
we can not plumb from ledges
the depths which lurk below
only falling gives up data
enough to judge the act
f)
fear is the structure
on which the course is scribed,
all movements drive the tension
in this zone of the web;
lines mutate to steel
and wires which slice our nights

GONE TO THOSE ENDS

1
what dreams are left?
our time shatters
we break down in decay
frantic and spastic
repeating actions of the past
which have fallen from all meaning
spraying out intention
which has an aim no more

2
these things of old intrigue us
they seem so present
their words reach to our life
as though for us alone
and not another age...
how do we reach these,
or their successors,
new teachers of the light?

3
sickness grasps
illness insinuates
changes course of day
makes all things hard
unable to attain
enforces patterns
of downward runs to death
upon dimensioned forms

4
we wait for echoes
from dear calls to the night
but sample silence
in staring disbelief
what lies beyond here?
what forms move through that dark?
our screens show nothing,
an absence that would damn

5
sands shift slowly
in gravity's demand
we cannot frame
a structure that will last
against this slippage
a bulwark to resist
the sinking cycle
which drains our soul away

PAIN AMASSED IN SINKING

what returns here?
these systems are familiar
yet we are still blind

the line is not enough
to reach the bottom of these cliffs
and save us all from drowning
in this cruel and sudden storm

such frustration
such brutal need
we can not grasp the diamond
which offers in our dreams
no matter how we ache

which cycles now?
we, too, would flee
but are chained herein,
no distance gives us solace
and few are offered
in horizons that we see

the battles hurry near
we are eclipsing
like shadows eating light
and dragons in the sun
no fortune smiles here
no goodness grows
within this tide

futile gestures
all these frantic acts
we know that doom is
the final scripted scene
and that these blockings
just move us ever on
to that destruction
the crushing of the end

those questions surface
and we have answers still
but wonder silent
how everyone denies
what seems so blatant
the open naked sore
which oozes darkness
and touches all the world
with the aspects of the lie

BROKEN ON THESE LINES

1
disassociation...
we are in different worlds
an alien space
this fulfils the vision
on a beach so long ago
but we don't fit here
any more than there

2
tides of darkness
sweep behind the scenes
touching high spots
with poison and decay

3
there is duty
which forms a drive
we split apart
schism in the mirror
portions taking the dull and tiring path
others dare to touch these skies with flight

4
something dies
responding to our willing
is driven off
by isolation
by our strength

5
strange disruption
absorbed by form
we gaze across those days
and wonder how they flow
and what they bring
hung between the abyss and the heights
hurtling being
into uncertain lots

6
know this name
stare into these depths
and stifle back your scream

INHOSPITABLE DAYS #4

here it comes
the toll again
the bells seem distant
so filled with change

what a broken time
this frame has been
we have no handle
no slight control
we drift so aimless
so wrecked by pain
and only are freed
in unreachable dreams

we take up chains
which have no end
yet peek around the edges
to see what lies beyond

here trace the lines
which mark our hands
this maps the way
our anguish travels
and perhaps points
into some future
which has not been foreseen
except beneath our sleep

we ache for that
but can not move
these systems falter
unredeemed

so much has shattered
and lurks in dread
a madness huddles
and threatens life
all loose ends wriggle
as though to strangle
wiping breath
away from form

tick tock tick tock
the hours move on slow
following a dirge
only space away

INHOSPITABLE DAYS #10

the twig snaps
the building falls
mountains collapse
seas leave their beds
to walk the land
as stars plummet down
in terrible storms
crushing everything below

aberrant systems rise
spinning out raw change
into what had been a stasis
we cannot consume
sufficient to survive
the trend is to decline
without a chance to brake
out of killer skids

new elements are dealt
into unseen stacks
we listen in the distance
aching to find clues
but can not decode patterns
with context for the self
in the murmured mutters
of data without frame

the currents do not shift
they still run back and dangerous
tainting inner states
that should have been evolved
by the chaos of the time
purged by shadows cast
by violence and mortality
so strong and hard to shake

transfer to new light
is the heart of desire,
it boils in the brain
like a dream obsessed;
tendrils of past need
weave into the mass
and convolute concepts
beyond what's attained

MOTIVE IN DEPARTURE'S ACHE

it slips by so fast
with so little to record
the visions tumble out
and we grasp so few
understanding
a smaller fraction yet

the structure presses us
but we don't touch the pattern
it hovers as a myth
a rumor whispered in back pews
that what has wrought the form
has forgotten how to fill

as capacity returns
intent becomes corrupted
we are twisted by our sources
and locked on inertia's grid
praying for old dreams
and reestablished states

time won't allow
these eyes to sate their greed
they have the wander ache
and pine always for the new
driving us for distance
which can not be achieved

we trace the lines of flight
scarring up the sky
almost tasting silver
in the drive to reach
what lies beyond horizons
deep behind the mind

what echoes from the past
to draw us to these depths?
we know how breaking comes
and see the omens at all sides
yet find this slope too steep
to ever craft return

GROUND IN CYCLED WHEELS

what can't be taken from vision
the tactile realm
so far away
alien in its normalcy

we can't break that line
all our weapons lost
in this isolation
banished from the homeland

we grasp too many tasks
piling tags on hours
killing futures with a grid
placed blindly in todays

there is an edge approaching
which opens onto chasms
storms hover over this
and blur the place of chaos

the oracle's dictated
that we can't jump from frames
and into other space and time
no matter how closely sensed

there is a mire which can't be broken
that locks us to this place
a thick confusion hazy
that slows all things to death

only dreams release us
from strictures of the real
the hard rule crushing
destroying every sense

what might survive of this?
all systems fail
and none foresee
the structures yet to dawn

BROKEN, BATTERED, IN DISMAY

each day brings new blasts
the decline continues
with folds on folds
convolutions to the plot;
we have no way to measure
the nature of the scheme
only counting the contusions
amassing on the soul

we can not reach
the land of need
we just see its horizon
on the far edge of the mind
it floats without directions
or definition to attain
tantalizing spirit
with the scent of deepest dreams

we ache to make these histories
known to all the world
yet blocks form at each juncture
and will not let us pass;
where might we find the sayings
to incant at each stage?
where are the hidden secrets
which would free us from all chain?

the system's wheels
grind closer still
the cutting teeth
rip at our flesh
we hoped to be away from this
we hoped the chaos fades
but these are of the cruelest times
and they focus on our pain

when all is lost
as it looks to be
when crashing comes
to abysmal depths
where can we go,
what can we do,
and what can change
the course of days?

THE PLACEMENT WHERE WE FAIL

so many things confusing now,
we can not build these pasts;
we pull in minimal examples
just enough to know
that there was a surface
which had been scratched

the mass is so great
we are unable to contain
the breadth of that existence
which we would bottle and display
in exhibitions of the horrors
which had once come to be

we drive against the pain
press on boundaries
defined by location
and the calendar's cruel grid
we falter in intents
and are left with vague pretense

these days go speechless
so many words must say
but fell to silence
our guilt spins scripts afar
without excuses to explain
how distant now we are

not enough is left
we harbor doubt within our fear
yet know the only truth
comes from the shady sides
not lit by doctrine's glare
or by the schedule's steel

we grow broken and not our own
we pass into the haze
where scents of ancient answers
drift by like menus set
for senses not yet framed
in context with the form

DROPPED INTO BLACKEST STATES

there is such a darkness fostered
within these places
we are at the center of the grid
the cross-hairs of destruction
all confusion feeds on us
and we are all consumed

nightmares embody
in madness organized
a sickness spreads all through the world
like poison crystals freezing
out of fluid states
which would allow a change

we are battered
abused by every day
our tears explode against these chains
as though to oxidize
but there's no freeing coming
no time of our release

lost are ancient powers
of exiting this plane
all our aspects are divided
and imprisoned in each state
unable to resettle
to what is coalesced

there must be breaking
the cosmos must be cleaved
to open up the doorway
that leads back to the land
which is the birthright
and destiny denied

this sanity confines us
these strictures grind us down
beneath the weight of crushing blindness
which has no knowledge
which bears no truth
and is the empty that we fear

PORTIONS OF DIRECTIONS SPED

1
there begins the void
we can not see its edge
but we can sense its zone
it piles on visions of the past
and taunts us for our dullness
in failing pattern
within the fourth dimension span
so plain before us

2
disturbing maths
churn before our eyes
we hear the echoes
of mocking disrespect
and wonder how deep
does this devotion go
in seeking out a pulpit
from which to antipreach

3
there are few allies
too many sleep
too many cloak themselves with lies
and make them doctrine
never to be dropped
less still be questioned
by heretics as I
so eager to unsettle

4
still the dream
will not allow the "real"
still these prayers
have filtered out that dread
still this aching
drives on beyond these days
and makes us question
what has not been betrayed

WHEN THE EMPTY SEA IS GONE

one last time
within these walls
the dungeon's closing
the chains have rusted out
we set off strangely
into a night
which bears more questions than before
but does so with less knives

we never thought
the cage would fade away
this cauldron of frustration
the gilded frame of rage
here the mausoleum
in which we watched rot youth
here the crushing masses
of the killing grinding wheel

these doors they close tomorrow
perversely how we mourn
for patterns so ingrained
and systems we've maintained
there come new forms of madness
in this great and swamping wake
for nothing has a place now
and no action has a way

these are the nights of finishing
of sorting through debris
and trying to stitch vectors
from these sharp and glassy shards
which offer no direction
now that the mode is "out"
we have found escaping
but know not where we are

so many things are passing
so many things have died
we count ourselves among them
and all that we have clutched
in frantic flights from torment
in this so-ill-fitting case
which now slips into memory
and will soon be hard to trace

About This Collection[*]

Here we are again. This volume is something of a milestone as it is the 25th collection of my poetry (in various forms) to see print, and the second to appear under the aegis of Eschaton Productions.

As with my other recent releases in this format, the poems herein represent about 10% of my compositions over a two-year period, in this case 1992 and 1993. This particular book very nearly came out posthumously, my only having barely survived an automobile accident in the fall of '93. Many life changes have ensued, however, creating shifts in tides nearly as cataclysmic as those of 1985, some four of these collections ago.

Stress, it is the water that we swim in, it is omnipresent and so deep as to crush. This is the state of humanity, our true milieu. We frantically claw for escape, but are ensnared, we search out every door, but find no promise, we ache for new beginnings but encounter, "Always, The End".

- B.M.T.

* From the original 1994 "chapbook" edition.